Are you ready for a
NEW
BEGINNING?

Are you ready for a
NEW
BEGINNING?

You can be all you desire to be

Glenda "Skip" Vogel

Rev. date: 09/19/2016

To order additional copies of this book, contact:
Xlibris
1-888-795-4274
www.Xlibris.com
Orders@Xlibris.com
746865

DEDICATION

Above all, this book is dedicated to the love and caring of my children, who stood by me as together we grew through the time of our life crisis of my being single again.

In gratefulness, this book is dedicated to Pastor Phillip Epperson. He lovingly saw the need for help to the hurting single again people. He had confidence in me to become their leader.

And to the dozens of helpers the Lord provided to work with me. All of whom have remained close friends.

The work has been blessed by the support of my caring, plus the expertise, of my editor, Denise Gates. She is more than a business associate, she is a loving friend.

I have much to be grateful for; being surrounded by supportive and loving family and friends.

PREFACE

Things happen. Then it's time to take the next step. You find yourself single again. You were once married but it's back to being single again. It is a difficult time.

Maybe you are at a time and place in your life you recognize that it is time for a change. It is time for you to gather your thoughts and begin to move towards the person you have always wanted to be. You can be all you desire to be. Do it now.

There are ways, things you can do to grow through these times. I am going to help you do just that, grow through these times. I can be trusted to do that because I have been there. I have worked through to a better, fulfilled life. You, too, can become more than you have ever thought you could.

I went on to become the woman I always wanted to be. Three years after my divorce I entered bible school and became the founding director of a ministry for Single Again Men and Women. You will find your place too. Hundreds of success stories have evolved from this ministry. Tangents run off in dozens of directions.

Twelve years later, I went to the foreign field as a medical missionary and bible teacher.

Giving out, serving others, doing what I do best, what I love the most, that is part of the secret. My Passions? Nursing and missions.

First, you deal with what is happening right now. Putting off your decision to work through these feelings will hinder your growth to your progress towards your more fulfilling life.

Our first objective is to restore, repair a damaged marriage. If the deed has happened, some helps are needed to get lives back in order. .

You are not stuck where you are. There are brighter days ahead...let's get going!

You will become more than you think you are. More than what you are now.

This is not a self-help book. It is not something we work on our own and become better. There are real problems and situations that we need to address, and we do that by beginning with the Lord. We must have that relationship with Him. He is still on the throne, the throne of grace and mercy. We don't do this alone. The Father God has sent the Holy Spirit to lead, to direct, and to comfort us.

We find ourselves in a new phase of life. The things that were, have changed. They are no longer the same. What was, is no more. Things are now different. Not always are we talking about being single again; in every life changes and growth are needed to be addressed.

This is the time to ask the Holy Spirit to draw near to us, allowing us to understand what we need to do. It is also a time to ask for grace to have the knowledge of His will so that we may be obedient and become all He intended for us to be.

The first step is to learn/practice prayer. When we pray, the Lord gets most of the attention. He will help us to work through all that has happened. He will lead us to a new place, to the new person that we desire to be. He will lead us through all circumstances.

That is why we can say, "this is not a self help book". We are partnering with the Holy Spirit. We call for His wisdom to get us to the new person that we want to be. It is impossible by ourselves. With God, nothing is impossible.

Now, doesn't that encourage you? Nothing is impossible with God. He gives us strength, He gives strength to the weary and increases the power to the weak. (Isaiah 40:28,29) Can you use any of that?

We will work together and a beautiful life is yours. Again, it is a serious mistake to put off beginning your path toward your new life. The time is now. Don't waste this opportunity, and let's begin NOW.

Skip Vogel

TABLE OF CONTENTS

CHAPTER ONE

INITIAL STEPS TO THE NEW YOU
Be Honest, War Stories, Identify Yourself

DO YOU WANT TO BE HEALED? JOHN 5:6

It is time for you to look at where you are and to ask yourself, "Do I want to be well?" "Do I want to feel better?" "What can I do to make this happen?"

Have you been in this place long enough? Do you want to move on in your life to better days? Or…are you getting so much from where you are that you don't really want to move on? Your pain and situation is bringing you a lot of attention. Are you ready to give that up and move forward? Jesus asked the paralytic at the pool of Bethesda, having been an invalid for thirty-eight years, "Do you want to be well?" (John 5:6) Ask yourself this question. Give it some serious attention. "Do I want to be well?"

It is important that it is stressed at this point that God hates divorce, but does not hate divorced people. He cares very much for divorced people. It is important that it is stressed at this point that God hates divorce, but It is important that it is stressed at this point that God hates divorce, but intention was not for divorce but for marriages to last a lifetime. Yet, He graciously gives us the forgiveness and restoration that is needed. He is the God of second chances. Receive your second chance and be grateful.

There's no denying that going through a life crisis situation such as divorce or a separation from loved ones, brings along with it much confusion and pain. It is a crazy time of life. Mood swings may be wide and happen often without any warning. It is not the most emotionally stable time of our lives.

Anger may be severe. Do you have so much anger that it begins to interfere in your ability to function and even to think clearly? Is this where you are?

Do you ever think, "Will I ever feel good again?" Your feelings may represent a loss so enormous that you can expect to have some really depressing times. Maybe you think that no one has ever felt this bad or that you are the only one. These are not abnormal feelings. Believe me, You Will Feel Better.

This applies to anyone experiencing any loss i.e. (your home, your job, even your dog). There are things you can do. It's time to begin doing them!

It is important that you know, or at least accept as true until the time that you can know, that your life is not over. It has changed. It is not the way you originally planned but it is not over. Take a look at the bigger picture than today. There is time for you to change and to develop a purposeful and fulfilling life.

Why would you want to stay where you are? Take a step out from where you are. The Red Sea did not part until Moses stepped into the water! I'll help you take that first step.

You are the single most important person in moving you from where you are to where you want to be. You can, and will, form new relationships. You will be comfortable with them. New identities will be formed.

Release your struggle. Trust me, you will be able to function as a single adult. Best of all, the crazy time will be a thing of the past. In John 5:9 we read "And he began to walk." You, too, will rise and begin to walk, to begin to have a new life.

There are no short cuts to having a full and wholesome life. Regardless of how your life looks to you right now, a beautiful life can and will be yours. You can be sure of this. God has said so, and so it is.

Ask the Lord to reveal to you what you need to deal with. Pride? Priorities out of order? Seeking God and His ways is the beginning of rebuilding new life for you.

It is absolutely necessary to begin now to concentrate on yourself. If you are divorced, stop focusing on your exmate and his or her problems. You can do nothing about them. Haven't your experiences taught you that cannot change anyone else?

If drugs and alcohol were involved, did your nagging, pleading, yelling…did that change anything? Did that help?

Whatever it is that you have lost, you can go on. There's a better place for you. You do not have to live in this place of where you lost something that was important. Do something about it.

Whatever it is that you have lost, you can go on. There's a better place for you. You do not have to live in this place where you lost something that was important. Do something about it. Now is the time to make a decision to move on and to grow.

Build dreams rather than focusing on the old broken ones. The rest of your life belongs to you. You can make better choices to improve your life. It is time to do something about you. Do the best that you can for right now.

There is no advantage in dwelling upon your past failures and shortcomings. Get up and get going toward better days and a better you. Be determined. Put some focus on your strong points, your strengths; not just your weak points. See yourself differently. You can choose to rise above things you have no control over. You can choose to walk in the heavenlies while you are still on earth.

Take a careful look at yourself, not to blame or shame, but to see where you are. What has happened? Do you have conflicting feelings? Sad and glad? Frustrated and peaceful? It is possible you feel more than one way, and at the same time. Ask yourself: "Where am I?" "Where do I want to go?"

Don't even try to do this alone. "Let go and let God" is a saying moto many groups have used for many decades. It works for you right now.

BE HONEST...and discover yourself.

Being honest with yourself is the first step. As you acknowledge the reality of your loss, you are in a position that allows God to work with you. He will position you so that you can get on with your life. He does not desire to blame or shame you.

Many of us have fallen short of our goals and expectations. Learn from your past failures.

Until you are honest with yourself in dealing with what really happened and are honest about yourself, you are still playing games and growth cannot take place. More about game playing later. Exactly what do you need to deal with?

In your attempt to be honest with yourself, it is vital that you avoid self-pity. Let it be enough for now for me to warn you of the destructive force that self-pity is. It keeps you locked into the situation and the problem,. It keeps you looking backwards, not forward. It keeps you being a victim.

Are you remembering that first we seek God and His ways? The only place to begin is to ask God for help. The bible is full of reports of failures when men of God forgot to seek God first. Moses, David, many of the great men of faith had their moments of failures too.

Well-meaning people will feed your pity. "You poor thing, you have had it so bad." "What a terrible thing you have lost." And maybe that's true. It is a terrible thing that has happened.

If someone came to you with a knife in their back, merely consoling them falls short of helping them. True compassion is taking the knife out; dealing with the reality of identifying the hurt and pain and being careful and gentle. Would you do less for yourself? Take the knife out, compassionately.

The Bible calls this honesty: confession. Confession is not just reciting our wrongs. It is taking ownership. "I own my past behaviors, reactions, the good and the bad". Ownership is what we're talking about.

Identifying your own past wrongs does not mean you condone them or that you will keep them. You simply know what you have done and are making the decision to keep these thoughts, actions, or you are exchanging them for something better. You no longer are living in this time or space. You have already moved on.

Do you need an example? How about sneaking around going to unhealthy places? You have identified that wild place as unhealthy and you have chosen not to go there any more.

Changes have begun to take place. You are disciplining yourself to make better choices, one at a time. The important thing is that you begin.

Forgive yourself if you need to. Identify what happened, forgive yourself, and put the new plan into action. Just be honest in identifying your own thoughts and actions.

However uncomfortable as it may be to say that you are divorced or acknowledge whatever you have lost, the truth is you are single. You have had a loss. It is where you are right now. Where you are is not a bad place to be. You can start to grow from there. It is the first step of honesty. Accept the place of where you are.

Before you can start off in a new direction, you have to find out where you are. What direction should you travel?

Which way? Everyone wants to get through the pain of a loss. The destination is very clear, but often times we are lost because we do not know where we are right now. Where are we...Single? Identity shattered? Big loses?

Being honest with yourself allows you to know the direction for you to go. Begin from where you are and move toward where you want to go. Take one step at a time. Being broken is not the end. Our God is the Creator God. He is not only a repairer of brokenness, He makes brand new.

You are the person who can help yourself the most. Take a look at the pain and inadequacies that you are facing as well as your strong points.

Would it help now to take time to write them down? No one needs to see the list except yourself, and you need to see it.

You have already found some things that you did not loose. You are still a parent, a son, daughter, an employee or business owner, a friend. Your new experiences that you are developing are adding to your identity.

You can create new experiences based on what you discover about yourself. An example would be your love for sports. Becoming single did not change your love for sports. That has not been lost. It's still there.

I have always enjoyed taking pictures. Desiring to do better work, I enrolled in three photography classes at a community college. Result? I was able to mat and sell my pictures just before I went to the mission field. The mission field was a dream I have had my entire life. After bible school, my church supported me and I went to Honduras, Central America for 10 years. I realized my dream. I did not loose that.

That photography class proved beneficial in several ways. I framed many of the pictures and gave them as gifts. I was the photographer at four weddings. It was a great help on the mission field. It helped me to see myself in a new light. It gave me success when I needed it most.

It's time to stretch out into something new, time to make your move. You, too, can become the person you know you are. There are many songs unsung still inside you.

There are things you didn't have time to do. Can you do them now? When was the last time you read a novel? Are you too busy? You don't have enough time to read? Maybe selecting a short story is the answer for you.

The important thing is for you to be honest in recognizing where you are now and doing something, however small, about it. If you have more time now, use it to your advantage.

However difficult it is to do anything at all, force yourself. Have a friend help you. Isolating yourself is not the help you need. Isolation and withdrawal may cause you to make some bad decisions or may even immobilize you into doing nothing at all. Your friends will enjoy being with you again, once you stop rehearsing about your divorce. Your friends have probably heard all there is to say.

WAR STORIES

It is time to lay aside the war stories you have been rehearsing. They are a way of tying you to the past, hindering you from going forward. They make us feel as if we are getting better, even though we are staying stuck in the situation. The truth is that all the energy is being spent on the past rather than on the present. You are focusing on the wrong target.

Reliving your past hurts keeps you stuck. Even if that person continues to behave in the same way towards you, such as rejecting you, not speaking to you, ignoring you, you have begun to move past these times. You are in charge of yourself. Don't allow others to control your feelings. That is not to say their hurtful actions don't hurt. It is to say that you have moved past them. You are on a new path. You are reaching out past where you were toward new places.

This is something that we develop our entire lives Retired people reach out and begin to do something they have not done before. It is an on going process. For you, this will take you from your place of hurt.

War stories keep you playing the victim. We must live in an environment of no victims, only victories. People feel sorry for you if you portray yourself as a victim. You can tell your story about what happened, and how you felt. Once that is done, then get on with the rebuilding of your life.

Look to the place where you want to be instead of the place where you were. God has a plan for every life. Sometimes our choices separate us from His plan. We need to ask His forgiveness and ask for directions for the new life to come. He is faithful to offer ways and means to our life, to our wholeness, to our growth.

God's love is unconditional. We can be thankful that we do not have to earn His love. Our debts have been paid in full regardless of our feelings of unworthiness or failure.

Are you willing to grow through whatever it takes to get to that place of wholeness and holiness that we are seeking?

Asking for help is not a sign of weakness. Now is not the time to be on your own. This is not the time for "I'm handling this just fine." "I am strong enough to make it through all this by myself." It is only human to need the help of others. Allow them to help you.

Shared burdens are lighter to carry. Others may have learned things you may not have learned yet and are willing to share with you. Our help, our growth, comes in community along with our reliance on the Lord.

Our help comes in community, not in isolation. Being vulnerable and admitting our weaknesses is scary, but take the risk. The rewards are great. You have now come a long way. You have accepted that you need some help.

Just a side comment. Are you using the blank pages to write what you are feeling, what is happening, new ideas, projects? The blank pages are there for a purpose. Use them. It's like journaling, to be seen only by you.

IDENTIFY YOURSELF...WHO ARE YOU?

Rather than allowing the events in your life to tell you who you are; mother, brother, doctor, look beyond the titles and begin to make life's circumstances and situations opportunities for you to grow. Past experiences, happenings, things you have done, these do not give you identity today. We are moving past that. I am no longer the Operating Nurse, I am something different now.

God has forgiven you and is helping you to move forward. What a wonderful place for you to be in.

Our identity comes from God, our Creator. Who/what owns you? We belong to Him. It is the very thing that owns us that gives us our identity, our worth. Does your job own you or your money or your position? What owns you? You are more than Mr. So and So's administration assistant.

Identifying yourself, who you are and what it is that you do, requires some time for introspection. When you identify yourself, what do you think about? There are the obvious things such as those listed above, as well as friend, employee, neighbor, nationality, church leader. Those things continue on after your divorce. Things are not as you planned and hoped for after your loss. All these things do in part identify you, but there is more. Be the best friend, the best brother, whatever that you can be.

If you have been married before, everyone seems to want you to be married again. It is as if you are not complete being single. Not so! The good news is that you are all right being single. You are whole. You are not a half a cookie, not a left over. You are complete being single. Any problems that you have do not stem from singleness. Your life is not in a hold pattern, waiting to be married. You may want to be married. That's okay too. However, your life goes on. You become stronger until the time you do remarry. You are not standing around until them.

You are a person of promise and ability. You have skills. You are formed and empowered by God Himself. Your season of singleness provides you a rare opportunity to grow in relationship with Him, to serve Him, without distractions. We live and serve in the now. It is non-productive to wait around for Mr. or Mrs. Right to come along. Apart from any romantic relationships, God wants to use you, as you are now. If your past is holding you back, let it go.

We learn to like the person we are with when we are alone. Another person is not needed to make us happy or to feel complete. It is too much of a burden to place on anyone. Enjoy your friends and family. You are a part of a really good thing. You can be alone or with others. You are complete all by yourself.

What is it that guides you? What is it that you seem to be thinking about all the time? Do you think of that person that is no longer with you? Do you focus on what happened all the time? Release those thoughts. The past does teach us many things but the past is not where we want to live.

These things, this way of thinking, they are non-productive. They sap your energy, your joy, and prevent you from getting on with your life. They cause you to be so taken up, so consumed. They bind you. They own you. You are not in control of yourself. These thoughts are in control of you. You must be in control of you, not something outside of yourself. Jesus and you can take care of your life. There is nothing too hard for the two of you to do. Amen?

Now the question is: "How do I use this new found identity?" Don't just believe it, act like you believe it. Stop rehearsing your ills and troubles. Live in the victory that is yours. Stop being a victim. Choose not to be a victim.

You can rely on the grace of God to see you through to your victory. Being free in Jesus frees that past from being in control of you. You need not be immobilized with the fear of making mistakes or being a failure, unwanted, or second best. You are not second best in God's eye.

Don't let the word "singleness" get in your way. Singleness is not second best to being married. It is just a different marital status. Enjoy where you are. God may change it, who knows?

My daughter recently gave me a picture of a kitten looking in a mirror and seeing a great lion. The caption said, "What matters most is how you see yourself." I hung this in the bathroom, next to the mirror. Everyday it is among the first things I see.

In the 1950's there was a political comic strip called Pogo. Pogo said, "We have met the enemy and it is us." Would you tolerate a friend who treated you the way you sometimes treat yourself?

You are to live in the now, preparing for eternity. Have you accepted Jesus, God's Son, as your Lord and Savior? Have you recognized your sinfulness, confessed, accepted your forgiveness? Have you accepted Jesus as the Christ? Then you have taken the first step towards preparing for eternity. Now you are to walk with the Lord, directed by the Holy Spirit who has come to live within you. Congratulations? You are on your way to heaven.

Remember who you are. Remember how special you are. Your potential, your capabilities, be all you desire to be, and do it now.

Before we go any further we must address the issue of your relationship with Jesus Christ.

Have you recognized that you are a sinner?
"All have sinned and fall short of the Glory of God."
Romans 3:23

Do you know that there is a penalty for sin?
"For the wages of sin is death." Romans 6:23

Jesus died on the cross, forgiving us for our sins.
"Christ loved us while we were yet sinners." Romans 5:8

What we need to do. "The gift of God is eternal life through Jesus our Lord." Romans 6:23

"For whosoever shall call upon the name of the Lord shall be saved."
Romans 10:13

We cannot do this ourselves. "For by grace are you saved through faith; and that not of yourselves: it is the gift of God: Not of works, lest any man should boast." Ephesians 2:8,9

Once you accept that Jesus has paid for your sins, you have confessed and accepted His sacrifice, accept his forgiveness. Invite Him into your life as your savior. This is called being "Born Again".

Now, find yourself a good bible teaching church. This is just the beginning.

NOTES

Chapter Two

HANDLING GRIEF AND LOSS
Shock, Denial, Anger, Bargaining, Depression, Acceptance

"COMMIT YOUR WAYS TO THE LORD."
PSALM 34

Experiencing a loss causes grief. It can be a loss of many different things. Your loss could be a spouse, a job, your house, money, or belongings.

It is important that you address your loss and your grief. Use the proper words to name your loss. Identifying what you have lost is as important as identifying what you have left. Ignoring your loss will not make it go away.

Although grief is a normal reaction to loss, it is difficult and uncomfortable. Craziness almost seems to become expected. Grief is the normal reaction to a painful situation.

Elizabeth Kubler Ross has done extensive research on the subject of handling grief. Her book, "On Death and Dying", is an excellent resource for study. She has described five stages that grief progresses through. The stages do not follow a constant pattern. You may repeat one stage or another or skip a stage all together only to return to that stage at another time. The important point to remember is that handling grief is a process. It is not a singular event. It does not happen all at once. It does not progress in an orderly fashion. Periods of grief can present a very trying time in your life. If you have experienced a loss, you have experienced grief.

Divorce is one of the most disturbing emotional states a person can endure. You can expect wide emotional swings, sleep disturbances, as well as eating disorders. Your entire system is affected. You may even wonder if you will ever feel good again. There has been a breaking of the bond with a person once loved. This hectic time is irrational, emotional, and may be desperate.

You are not meant to go through grieving alone. A confidant is needed. Someone you can trust. Seek competent counseling from a trained person, a person familiar with the Word of God and what God has to say about these matters. This is not a time to drift away from Him. This is a time to draw closer to Him, the source of your strength and direction.

Becoming a part of a Christian group for support will help. You are able to share experiences. I thought that something that had happened in my family was unique and that no one else had to deal with something like this. I never told anyone. I felt misplaced shame or shame for something someone else had done. Imagine my surprise to learn that others in the group shared that same experience. The shame left. I was able to move on. Could this be your story, too?

There are many heavy feelings involved such as anger, emptiness, loneliness, hurt, confusion, and bitterness. We will deal with each of these feelings later.

SHOCK

A frequent beginning, as described by Dr. Ross, is shock. Shock does provide a temporary emotional distance so we can address what is happening more slowly. Shock is normal and automatic. It is a safeguard, buying us some time as we try to grasp the significance of what is happening. Symptoms of shock happen whether you caused what happened or someone else did,.

Hardship and disaster rarely give us time to prepare. Consider Job and how quickly he lost everything. Shock over what has happened, and is happening, may be your first line of defense. It is giving you time to think and to gather the facts. It is a time to examine yourself. What have I done to encourage this situation? When death has occurred, simply accepting the permanence of the separation may take some time.

DENIAL

Closely following shock, and many times along with it, is denial. "This can't be happening to me." "I didn't do anything so bad." The feeling of unreality surrounds the realization that the relationship is in danger of breaking up or has already broken up.

Denial, refusing to face up to the new reality, can be expressed in many ways. Some people simply refuse to accept it, thinking, "It isn't happening." "Things will be different soon." They will avoid the subject or will not discuss the loss or make any moves to address it in any way.

Another way of expressing denial is to minimize the importance of what is happening. "He or she will come around soon." "It will be better tomorrow."

People may become involved in various activities that keep them from experiencing the pain of their loss. Or they may choose to see only a small part of the picture with insufficient information. They may become overly involved with another activity i.e. work, school, ministry.

No matter how you address your grief, it is rarely dealt with quickly. It is a process and it takes time for changes and growth to occur. There is great danger in postponing dealing with the realities of the circumstances of our grief. It is painful. It is not anything you want but the fact is that this is happening or has happened.

Grief may immobilize you. I sat for two days in a cold house with no furnace until God sent a friend, someone I barely knew, to come to see me. She took care of things, including calling for a repairman. Since this was something that my husband always did, and he was no longer there. I was immobilized. I know this sounds ridiculous but these things do happen.

Getting over grief is not a test of faith. It is not a sign of weakness or a lack of faith. There is a need to draw upon the Lord. Those who cut themselves off from God are cutting themselves off from the very source of their nurturing, their strength. In the face of such tragedy, we must have the hope and assurance that a relationship with the Lord gives to us.

We have family and friends to be there with us also. They are a great source of help. Remember, our help is in community. Encourage one another to seek the help of the church and community groups.

"I am the vine, ye are the branches, He that abides in me, and I in Him, the same brings forth much fruit, for without me ye can do nothing." John 15:5

The point is there is no security apart from God. Our relationship with Him, the comforter, the healer, is the one relationship we have control over. We have as much of God as we want. He has given all to everyone. It is our responsibility to take what He has given. Our best recovery is dependent upon our relationship with God.

ANGER

Anger comes unexpectedly and is hard to control. God has given us a full range of feelings, and one of them is anger. It is neither righteous nor unrighteous. What we do with our anger may end up being righteous or unrighteous. Anger is a God-given feeling. It is a signal.

Anger is a signal that something is happening. What is it? Denial of angry feelings is both unhealthy and unproductive. To deny your anger is to deny the real problem. Sooner or later you will have to deal with the source of the anger and then deal with the anger itself.

What happened? How do I feel? What can I do to feel better? What constructive things can I do to make the situation better? Recognize your anger. Express your anger in a healthy way that will not cause you to sin. "I am angry. It is okay" Using a baseball bat to pound someone to express your anger is not okay.

I have heard it said, "True Christians are never to feel anger." The message here is that it is a sin to feel anger. This is not only theologically inaccurate, it is also impossible. God has created us with a full range of emotions, and one of them is anger.

How unreasonable to expect anyone to be happy and joyful all the time, especially when going through major changes, a personal loss, or living in a crisis situation. We are told to be happy, smile, and act as we think we would if we were really happy. Other people can deal more easily with our joy, but not with our sorrow.

Identify your actual feelings: "I am angry." Learn to deal with your feelings by removing the unrealistic goal of being happy continuously. Sometimes you are happy, but often times you are not. Then, find out the source of your anger. Give it a name. Decide what you can do to make the situation less angry. You need to accept the things you cannot change and change the things you can. I am angry because....sometimes it's right, and sometimes it is not, but you must own the anger.

A useful, attainable, and healthy goal is to be at peace with yourself. You will not have to pretend anymore. Be honest with yourself. In addressing your anger, admit that you are angry. You are in a place now to see what to do about this. Admitting your anger was a strong, positive step. This is the time to seek the direction of the Lord. Ask Him for His way of handling your situation.

Begin to look for healthy, constructive ways to work out your anger. Join a gym. Work up a sweat. Do something for a noble cause. Engage in some physical work. Give something a big piece of your attention and do your best to make it a success. Start making a list of possible things you can do. Be creative.

Some community activities may help you in working out your anger. Keep a journal so you can write down what you are feeling. It will be for your eyes only. Join a support or recovery group. You will immediately find out that you are not alone. There are many like you who are feeling the same way that you are feeling.

Let the anger go. It is a choice to move past the hurt so that it is not allowed to dominate and control your life. It is not to say you don't hurt anymore. You are just releasing the anger. Time does not heal, but it does take time to heal. It's better not to be angry during this time. The goal is always to move past the hurt. You begin to move beyond the hurt when you let go of the anger. Forgive yourself and others as well.

It is time to leave the past, to live in the present. It is time to get on with the rest of your life. What do you say? Is it worth the effort?

Blaming yourself for not being able to change the past course of events is self-destructive behavior. It leads to feelings of powerlessness. Someone else is in charge of you and how you feel. You can, however, be in charge of accepting your part of the responsibility for the breaking of a relationship, asking God's forgiveness and guidance to learn a new way of behavior, and moving forward with God.

"Commit your ways to the Lord." (Psalm 34).

BARGAINING

Dr. Ross tells us that it is not unusual for those dealing with grief to enter into a period of bargaining. This is a nonacceptance stage. It is a stage of "What if?" Bargaining is a final try to take control of your life. It is a last ditch attempt to control life so you can get your own way. Even Job wanted his "day in court." (Job 23). He thought if only he could explain to God, God would deliver him.

"If only" thoughts are not helpful. Asking yourself "if only I had done or said something differently" These thought are not helpful. They are a way that a superficial sense of hope may develop. Most "if only" statements are not really true. Your behavior is separate from anyone else's. They are in charge of themselves just as you are in charge of yourself.

If your feelings of regret and guilt are based on genuine misdeeds, there is nothing to do except to confess such things, ask for forgiveness and make any amends that you can.

It is the wrong view of God to think that He is able to be manipulated. God is sovereign. The closer you choose to be to God, the quicker you will get to acceptance and to be able to move forward in your life. A brighter horizon is there for you.

DEPRESSION

Depression may follow bargaining. In depression, everything seems to come to a stop. Some very heavy emotions are present and affecting daily life; perhaps despair, loneliness. Physically you may have weight gain or loss. You may cease to care about your personal appearance or seek isolation. It is not a time of clear thought and accurate perception. "Why bother?" "Who cares?" There are many questions and very few answers.

However, the beginning of rebuilding your life can be found here. You have taken your first look at the fact that your life is changing. Your defenses are breaking down. The reality of your loss begins to sink in deeply. It may dominate you, even crush you. The sense of hopelessness and powerlessness to change anything may seem overwhelming.

There is no normal time frame for depression. Depression may reoccur when a song, a sight, etc. that rekindle memories. Grief may keep coming back with various degrees of intensity and for various lengths of time. There is no usual time for handling grief and its many faces.

To deal with depression you must begin to let go of the past. Develop a self-identity that is not locked into what has been lost. You are your own person. Do you know who you are and what it is that you do? Work from that spot. Work from what is left and continue toward what can be.

You can help yourself and let others help you, too. Talk to them. Remember that you are not meant to handle your grief and loss by yourself. Pray with someone. Enjoy their company. Healing comes in community, not in isolation.

Reduce the time of your healing by sharing feelings on a regular basis with a significant other. It is better if it is a friend of the same sex. This is not the time to begin another serious relationship.

Allow someone to help you, someone who will keep your confidence. Be wise in selecting this person. Read the Word of God, the Bible, everyday, especially the praise psalms. Rejoice and be comforted in the love and support of God's Word.

Face the facts squarely with all of their pain. Do not allow yourself to sink into inactivity. Parking yourself in front of the TV and becoming mindless is a sure way to remain in depression.

Are you seeing that there are many things you can do? It takes energy to decide not to do something just as it takes energy to do something. You know what to do. Decide to do it.

Is doing nothing your standard way of coping? Doing nothing to resolve the crisis feelings only increases your feelings of being trapped. If you see the need, then do what is necessary. Face your resentments, forgive the unfairness. Get on with the good things in your life. You are in charge of your thoughts, your actions, too.

We are physical, emotional, and spiritual beings. Are you taking care of yourself? Getting enough sleep and rest? Are you eating properly? Exercising? Or do you live regularly with fatigue? If you do, you are guaranteed depression. Get up off the couch and do something about this.

We are not above the laws of nature. Balance your life; you do not need to live above realistic possibilities. If you need to slow down, slow down.

Although the above may not be the immediate problem in your life, if you continue to abuse yourself physically, your depression will be even more difficult to treat.

ACCEPTANCE

With acceptance comes the beginning of your ability to reach out again. Life is going to go on and you have decided to join it. You are a special person in charge of your own life. It is the time when you take positive steps to make tomorrow just a little bit better than today was.

Acceptance does not mean that the pain is all gone. Acceptance is a state of emotional balance. It is a realization that life is not over, it has only changed.

Acceptance does not mean that you like the things that have happened to you. It means that you have stopped fighting the inevitable and are trying to adapt to the new ways with grace and dignity. You are moving on with your life. You have expressed your willingness to live on even with your pain, holding onto God as the source of comfort.

Acceptance does not mean other people's behavior will change. It merely means that you are aware of what has happened. You cannot change anyone else. You can only change yourself.

Resignation is negative and passive. It carries with it the seeds of self-pity and self-imposed martyrdom. Acceptance is looking up into God's face with love and trust, allowing Him to choose for you. It is a trust issue.

You can declare, "I believe in the grace of God to see me through this situation."

NOTES

CHAPTER THREE

DEALING WITH HEAVY FEELINGS
Facts or Feelings, Thinking or Feeling

"I HAVE LEARNED THE SECRET OF BEING CONTENT WHATEVER THE CIRCUMSTANCES." (PHILIPPIANS 4:11).

From the beginning, you must understand that feelings are not facts. Because you feel a certain way does not make it so. It may not be truth. Because you feel you have lost all your friends does not mean you have lost all your friends. You are feeling that you have.

What are feelings then? Feelings are merely signals. A sign that something has happened. Light feelings, heavy feelings, are all signals that something has happened.

What is it that happened? If you feel, you feel something. What is it that you feel? By expressing your feelings and giving them a name, you take the first step in dealing with feelings. It helps to clarify your thinking when you identify your feelings. Give them their names.

Knowing the difference between feeling and thinking does help. Thoughts are not the same as feelings. Thinking and thoughts have to do with understanding the facts and information.

You think things are not going well. You do not feel things are not going well. You may feel sad that things are not going well. Feelings are not facts. They are not information.

When I was in the choir and the director said for us to line up according to our height. I would always head for the medium tall ladies, 5'6". Just as regularly, the director would smile and point to the short ladies. Because I think of myself as average height does not make me average height. The fact is I am 5'3" and that is among the short. Feelings and wrong thinking did not make it so.

You need to understand the difference between feelings and thinking to better understand how to use feelings to your advantage. It will help you to make better decisions and better choices in rebuilding your life.

Your feelings are your own. They belong to you. How you feel about something is how you feel. It doesn't matter how anyone else feels about the matter. You feel a certain way. Because the feelings are yours, you are the one who must learn to deal with them.

Most people easily accept joy, a lighter feeling. It is sadness and depression that people have a harder time accepting. We have to deal with joy, too.

We need to take note here about the children. Children have the same feelings that you have. As you become well, in more control of your feelings, the children will too. They also feel the loss. They are scared, sad and wonder what life is all about. They wonder what is happening to them. Their thinking and feelings are confused, too.

Sometimes, they feel that they are responsible for what has happened. It is unrealistic, but they may think that if they had done something differently, what has happened would not have happened. Allow the children to admit to their feelings, act them out, and express them. They need the opportunity to talk, too.

You can expect to have some really down times during the recovery from a personal loss. The loss may be enormous. Even though you feel you are the only one to experience such pain at such a loss; that is not the fact.

You are not unique. You will one day feel better. Give yourself the time it takes to heal, to work through the process of your recovery toward a brighter horizon.

Feelings are not facts, remember? They signal that something has happened.

One good thing about these heavy feelings is that they can motivate us to act. Feelings exist to direct us toward facing our problems and to make the necessary changes.

Feelings are directors. They are not suppose to control us. However, they will control us if we allow it. Rise above them, be all that God has intended for you to be.

Trust the Holy Spirit. He is the director. He will help you in your confusion. Consider the following: "Seek God and His Ways." (Matthew 6:33).

Seek a balance in your life. You are a spiritual, physical, and emotional being. Nourishment is needed in all three areas. It is not wise to ignore any one of these areas.

When you forgive, you are given peace. People have the bigger problem when they do not forgive. Your responsibility lies only in your own behavior, only in what you choose to do.

A change in attitude may be in order. Change from a negative to a positive life style. Emotional growth from anything requires a decision and a determination to grow and change. If you continue as you are, how can you expect anything short of what you already have? It is the craziest of crazy to do the same things and to expect different results.

If you make the same kind of decisions, same choices, keep the same attitudes, rehearse the same negatives about yourself, other people, your job, how can you expect to think or to feel any different than you do? It is the craziest of crazy! (Are you using the note sheets to write your feelings?)

Use your energies to rebuild your life, dealing with reality. Truth will untie you from the circumstances. Start from where you are. Let the past go. The future is coming.

How are you to do this? Increasing your prayer life is a good place to start. It will begin to heal many memories, hidden hurts, and anger. Tell God you are willing to forgive, willing to be forgiven, and willing to let God change your feelings.

Incorporate this thought into your daily prayer life: "Lord, I really want to change, to forgive, to be more like you. Help me, show me how to be all you desire of me."

It may be a struggle, but it is worth the effort. All labor produces profit. How can you grow if you are stuck in your heavy feelings? God's love washes away hurt, anger, and unfairness. Face up to your true feelings and resolve them in the understanding of His love.

Here are some ways of meeting the problem of heavy feelings:

1. When necessary, force yourself to be with other people. This is one of the major areas where you have a definite choice. You need community at this time, and not isolation.

2. Seek help from others. Your perceptions change during depression, mole hills become mountains. Seek people who generate joy. You have the choice.

3. Sing and make music. In 1 Samuel 16:14-23 the beauty of David's music lifted King Saul's spirit of depression. Would music do any less for you? Your choice here is to select joyful, pleasant, uplifting music.

4. Praise and give thanks. Ephesians 5:20 reminds us to remember and to be thankful. "Giving thanks always for all things unto God and the Father in the name of our Lord Jesus Christ." Paul does not say feel thankful for everything. Paul says to give thanks for everything.

5. This is the time to lean heavily on the power of God's Word. The book of Psalms is used with great frequency as an aid in encouraging and lifting up our spirits.

6. Rest confidently in the presence of God's Spirit. "Hope thou in God, for I shall yet praise Him for the help of His countenance." (Psalm 42:5).

"The times of refreshing come from the presence of the Lord." (Acts 3:19).

Are you beginning to see that the scriptures have planned out the way for you to go even before you could ask? The answers to your questions are in God's book.

It is accepting a myth to believe that Christians cannot be depressed or experience heavy feelings. Consider David in Psalms, Elijah, Jonah and even Jesus in Matthew 26:38. "My soul is exceeding sorrowful, even unto death."

If you deny your heavy feelings, you add guilt to your feelings by saying, "There is something wrong with me, I am depressed." You have then doubled the weight causing an impossible load to carry.

However, if you have sin in your life and you have not addressed this issue, you add much confusion. You must ask for forgiveness and change your ways before you can develop a true and loving relationship with God.

You do not get a new personality when you seek forgiveness and a relationship with God. You do learn tools of refining your ways. You learn to put aside the old man, and to put on the new man. Accept the personality that you have. You can allow the Holy Spirit to be in control of you and in helping you to break old, bad habits or ways of responding. The love of God is not grounded in your feelings or performances but in His faithfulness.

Allow the Lord to lift you above what is happening. Think upon better things. "Whatsoever things are true, whatsoever things are honest, whatsoever things are just, whatsoever things are pure, whatsoever things are lovely, whatsoever things are of good report; if there be any virtue, and if there be any praise, think on these things." (Phil 4:8).

Do you notice that not all things are true, honest, just, pure, lovely, of good report but whatsoever things are, you are told to think on these things?

NOTES

CHAPTER FOUR

ADDRESSING HEAVY FEELINGS
Rejection, Self-esteem, Positive thinking, Loneliness

"GOD IS NOT THE AUTHOR OF CONFUSION" II TIM 1:7

Let's take the opportunity to consider some common heavy feelings following the breakage of a relationship. Divorce or death of a spouse, both leave us with some very heavy feelings. Even if you have not experienced them, perhaps you can reapply the message to another area. It's worth your effort to continue on.

Being able to name your feelings, and then doing something to feel less pain, is recovery. It is feeling better, making the right choices towards a better life. There are things you can do.

"Put off the old man, put on the new man." Eph. 4:24

Keep in mind that feelings are just signals that something has happened. They can be directors helping us to make good choices.

REJECTION

Who has escaped the horrid feeling of rejection? Rejection of some sort has touched just about everyone. It is a feeling that reaches into the very soul of a person. It can eat away at all we believe about ourselves and leaves us bare, exposed for all to see. Rejection breaks down self-esteem.

When someone rejects you, they are refusing to accept you as a person. To refuse your kindness, intentions, or love is to refuse you. That is why rejection is so terribly painful and destructive.

Rejection implies that something is not right about you. You are not wanted. The team has been chosen, but not you, implying that you are not good enough. It may not be true, but the awful feeling is there.

To be cast away, discarded, not wanted or needed, can leave us with few admirable feelings about ourselves or about what is happening to us. If we are thrown away, are made to feel useless, unsatisfactory, what come next?

Unless attended to, rejection can be as a cancer eating away at the very life of us. It does indeed have the means to destroy our self-esteem and to render us immobile. But then, feelings are not facts, are they?

Perhaps someone has tossed you aside and is no longer wanting or needing your presence, does that make you rubbish? Consider that this says more about them than it does about you!

Once again, I urge you not to accept all the negatives and perhaps, even the lies that have come against you in the divorce process, or in any other happening in your life. You have no control over nastiness. You can only control yourself. Say to yourself, "I refuse to accept this nastiness." Recognize it as being apart from you.

The best you can do when you come against someone being nasty is to insulate yourself against what is said or done.

Insulating yourself is only a part of rebuilding your life. You do not have to accept another's nastiness. The initial response may be to quickly, physically, separate yourself. Walk away from the situation. Staying and quarreling is nonproductive. Walking away may give you an immediate good feeling; a release of anger or hurtful feelings.

One way to begin this insulating process is to put on the armor of God. Ephesians 6:10-17. Put on the Armor of God, all of it, everyday. The Lord is our protector. A dear friend of mine had a dream. God's helmet of salvation was filled with the blood of Jesus. As it was put on, the blood covered her from the top of her head to the bottom of her feet. Our most vital parts are covered by the breastplate of righteousness. We have that right standing with God.

Do you see the Father God fighting for us in this passage? "Out in front of us, our shield is God the Father." (Psalm 33:20). Our loins wrapped in truth, Jesus is that truth. (John 14:6) We are covered with Jesus Himself. The sword of the Spirit, it is the Spirit that attacks our enemy.

Remember whose child you are, the battle is the Lord's. When evil comes against us, the Lord comes into battle for us. During these roller coaster times, it is vital that we daily put on the armor of God so that we might fight against these attacks.

This is not the time to separate yourselves from God, as is the tendency of many. This is the time to draw close to Him. It does not matter that you do not feel like praying or conversing with God. The fact is that this is your best and only means of strength and clearness of thought. "God is not the author of confusion but of a sound mind." (2 Tim. 1:7)

SELF-ESTEEM

Since you are responsible for you, approval of yourself depends on you. What do you think of yourself? Others may voice another opinion but you do not have to depend on what they think, do, or say to feel good about yourself. Too long we have depended on what others in our lives think of us. How do you see yourself?

If you hear criticism and lies about yourself long enough, the tendency is begin to believe them. It is time to take a clearer look at yourself. You will make some wonderful discoveries.

You already know that you are a child of the King. You belong to God. You are made in God's image for greatness. "Let us make man in our image." (Gen. 1:26).

As a child of God, it is not necessary to go through life alone. He will accompany us through many relationships. It is God's strength that enables us to get through the tough times of rejection and loneliness.

"I can do all things through Christ who strengthens me." (Phil 4:14).

Don't just read it, behave like you believe it!

I am not encouraging denial of the truth, but of focusing upon lighter feelings and facts when things get really tough. As least until you have your feelings under control. It is difficult to rise above depressing thoughts with a shift of focus.

THINKING POSITIVELY

Look positively at the past. It was not all bad. Look positively at the present. Look positively at the future. It is time to look ahead with expectations of a better life. The new life is one of peace, of growth and productivity.

Learn to talk positively about yourself. List the positive things about yourself. Post it where you can see it. Speak those things to yourself. The more negative things you say to yourself, the more you will believe they are true. The same is true about the positive things that you say or think. You will believe them too. A large part of the problem is our self talk is negative.

I am speaking always of truth. Why do you say, "I am a failure?" You have not failed in everything. List your successes; your job, the love you have for your family, there are dozens of things you have done well. Think on those things. It is imperative that you shift your focus to a more positive stance.

Keep turning to God, you cannot handle all your problems alone. We need God and each other through these times and on to a brighter horizon.

By behaving in stronger, positive ways, whether we feel like it or not, our attitudes and beliefs about ourselves will begin to change. Our feelings will catch up to our behavior. It may take a couple of weeks, but keep practicing.

It is time to put 'the program' into practice. Service to others is a major way towards helping yourself as well. Keep active in worthwhile pursuits. Do something nice for someone; help someone out. Write a thank you note. Help out in a soup kitchen. Volunteer in a community service. There is an unlimited list of worthwhile things you can do for others.

There are things that you are really good at, or could be if you applied yourself. Is this the time for you to develop an interest you have always had? Be your best. Compare yourself only to yourself. Can I do better than I have done?" Develop your talents. The achievement will lift you above the put-downs and negatives that come your way during rejection.

During hard times with heavy feelings, try looking your best, smile, it lightens the load. Even in a house of tension, there is always room for one happy person. Play with the kids. Practice laughing out loud so you can hear yourself laugh! Yes, out loud. Hear yourself being happy.

On the telephone, a friend read to me a speech he was about to give at a meeting. It included a couple of jokes. I listened and smiled broadly. Because we were on the phone, he couldn't see that I enjoyed the stories. He said, "I guess I can't use these stories, you didn't laugh even once." I needed to laugh out loud!

I noticed my daughter and a special friend always laughed out loud. So I tried it too. I surprised myself. I had forgotten how I sounded. It was wonderful. I love to hear myself laugh. You will too. Put the program into practice. Tell a couple funny jokes. You don't know any? Memorize some. When I first tried this, my kids and I were out for pizza, quietly eating. They just looked at me, puzzled. Then after the second or third joke, we all laughed. They began to tell jokes. Laughing is so much fun. "A merry heart makes a cheerful countenance." (Proverbs 15:13).

There is a saying. "Fake it until you make it." Behave in a certain way until your feelings and attitudes catch up to your behavior. They will catch up; believe me. You have begun the rebuilding of your life.

"In everything give thanks; for this is the will of God in Christ Jesus concerning you." (I Thess. 5:18).

LONELINESS

The loss can be and usually is, so enormous following divorce or the death of a spouse, or separation, that you could expect some really down times during the entire ordeal. As you begin to rebuild your life, these down times will become shorter and shorter. Remember you are not the only one to experience such heavy feelings to such a depth.

Although at times it may feel like 'no one could have ever felt this bad!'

The pain connected with loneliness, having lost your companion, may be overwhelming. Loneliness is a feeling like any other and it is telling you that there is an area in your life that needs your attention. Something has happened. What are you going to do about it? Loneliness itself is not the problem. It is a symptom of an underlying problem.

As you search for and find what has happened, focus on that. If you are lonely, get into community. Join a group with similar interests. Don't forget to bring along your smile. Be positive. Yes, it may be difficult at first but as you practice being positive, smiling, it will become easier and easier. You will meet new people too.

Remembering that our healing comes in community and not in isolation, we readily see that the answer lies not in running away and hiding. Staying cooped up alone in a one bedroom apartment and working 50-60 hours a week is not the answer. Besides joining a group for support, examine your interest. What is out there socially for you? It is a way to meet other people and to get you out into the community.

Do something new for the moment. This is not to say it will become a life-long pastime. Perhaps it is just for now, while you are getting it all together again.

Certainly feeling sorry for yourself won't do you a whole lot of good. It may be true that you have been treated very unfairly. However, walking away from the past by redirecting your focus on more positive, productive happenings will make you feel better.

In today's life it is easy to get mood altering drugs, either by prescription or otherwise, on the street. They are not the answer. They are a temporary fix. We need permanent fixes. We need to rebuild our lives and move on to better, more wholesome lives.

Examine where you want to be and begin moving in that direction. Determine that you will seek after and as close to the life you desire as you can.

One woman I know enrolled in a correspondence course in the bible. It was the most helpful thing she did. A position opened up for her at her church. It saved her life for eternity and for her life here as well.

This is just another opportunity out there for you to examine and decide if taking a class in something new may be the perfect thing for you to do. One thing that seems to happen during this time is that the pendulum swings widely to the opposite ends. From isolation, you may overcompensate and become a social butterfly. Joining everything in sight is not the answer either.

As singles, we must learn that being alone isn't so bad. As you put your new program into effect and begin to get your life back into some kind of order, you will see that you have begun to like the person you are with when you are alone. The key here is to lead a balanced life.

Like overeating, overspending, going on a buying spree; they all are recognized as the symptoms of being lonely. There is a momentary high but it doesn't last and they bring along with them inevitable consequences. Extra pounds will have to be taken off, bills will have to be paid and new things get old and do not satisfy for very long.

Even though you have lost a relationship, new friendships, new relationships will be coming your way. As you get out in the community you will meet new people for your life.

NOTES

CHAPTER FIVE

BUILDING RELATIONSHIPS
Friendship, Belonging, Goals

"BEHOLD I AM WITH YOU ALWAYS."
MATTHEW 28:28

This is a new beginning for you. Let me remind you that your life is not over. It has changed from what you thought it would be. Consider what you have, who you are, and beginning there, move on. Live in the today. Make it better than yesterday.

Regardless of what has happened to make your life, as it is, your being lonely tells you that you are lacking relationships. It may be a relationship with God as well as with other people.

How well do you know God? Do you spend much love and time with Him? The Lord is your comforter, your strength, and your companion. He walks along side of you, is ever present.

Seeing that your relationship with the Lord is your most important relationship, the only one having eternal value, it makes good sense to develop that closeness with Him. Get yourself into reading the Bible, His Word. Learn about who He is and what He does. That should get you started.

To know Him is to love Him. If you don't feel much like reading and praying, begin by asking the Lord to help you get started. It will get easier as you progress with Him.

"For I the Lord God will hold thy right hand, saying unto thee, Fear Not. I will help thee." (Isaiah 41:3). What a promise! Receive it and be encouraged!

RELATIONS WITH FRIENDS

Loneliness also involves either an absence of friends or perhaps you may be neglecting those that you have. There are many people you know that may need your companionship as well as you need theirs. Make a list of people who you could call and encourage.

A sure-fire formula for winning the battle against loneliness is found in Galatians 5:13-14 "By love serve one another."

Loving and serving defeat loneliness. They allow you to forget yourself, and the present experiences, and to focus on something productive. Giving of yourself for even a few short hours allows you to be productive, stops you from reliving the past, and to begin living in the present. It becomes a practice session in moving forward instead of hanging on to the past.

You cannot serve only out of duty. It then becomes drudgery. You will soon feel unappreciated and that you are the victim. It is the same with your relationship with God. Our serving must be of a loving relationship as well.

FIND A PLACE TO BELONG

We all need a place where we can go and be a part of. Join a group with people of similar goals and interests. You like collecting coins? Join a coin collecting group. Be a working member of the group and contribute. Do not just expect the group to love and serve you.

If you are in a breaking relationship, find a recovery-support group. Many churches have such groups. They are safe groups for you to be a part. People of similar happenings, following the principles of biblical support, will be a really safe place for you to belong.

Give yourself some time to adjust to the group. Go several times to learn about it. Go with them to social events, especially things like coffee after a meeting.

Socialize with the group when they meet. What is planned may not be a high priority with you but attend anyway. Your presence in the group encourages others. Talk to the people and be as friendly as you can be. You be the encourager. They are hurting too.

There are things you like to do too. Suggest them. Work on that outing to make it as successful as you can. Be a participating member; let no job be too small for you to do. It is sometimes many times harder to do the small jobs rather than the bigger works. No one seems to notice the smaller works being done but for now, it may be easier for you to do them. These jobs need to be done too.

It is not productive to waste your energy on things that you cannot change. Direct you energy on being successful with the goals that you have set. Successful group experiences are a goal worth pursuing.

Enjoy the moment that you are in. If you return to a less joyful time, you still had the enjoyable earlier time, or the planned function to come. It is not profitable to dwell in the past unhappy time. Live in the moment you are in and work your plan to a better you.

Wanting another person in your life who will be there for you is not an undesirable desire. Generally we turn to someone of the opposite sex and demand too much from them too soon. We are too desperate and expect too much from such a relationship.

Expecting someone outside us to meet all our needs is unrealistic. You need to begin with yourself. When you are confident that you are taking care of yourself, then you just may perhaps be ready to look about for that special relationship that you think is missing in your life.

Before you can expect someone else to meet your needs, you will have to meet your own needs. Rebuilding your life is the first order of business. You cannot fill empty moments with instant relationships. That is one reason why over socializing does not work.

The solution lies in rebuilding your own life and developing a relationship with God, yourself, and others. At this time in your life; look for a strong friend of the same gender.

You learn to love not by telling yourself to love or by doing things. You learn to love by knowing. Learn to know your God, and your friends, and your family. We learn to love by knowing God loves us. Once you discover that you are loved, you then have the ability to love others and to serve as you love.

Once you have learned to love and care for yourself, then you can have a wholesome love for others. Each of us take our own feelings about ourselves into our relationships with others. We love because we feel good about ourselves, not because we expect a response of love from the other person. Your approval and love for yourself do not depend on anyone else.

Learn to be as positive and as mature as you can be for the place that you find yourself in at the moment. No one even suggests that you are in an easy place. Changing marital status for any reason is difficult, but not impossible. Feed the good and watch it grow.

One of the more difficult adjustments for me was going out for dinner, especially banquets. There was that empty seat next to me. The solution is to go with someone. Why go alone? That was easy.

Taking positive steps involves learning to know yourself better. Everyone has good points and points that need correcting and adjusting. Be as honest with yourself as you can be.

Perhaps your former spouse had a valid complaint about you. Do something about it. If you do not make an adjustment in what you are, you will repeat that characteristic. You will bring it into all your relationships including another marriage, which will be as damaged as the first marriage. All your friendships will suffer the same damage as well.

Examining yourself honestly and working on improvement will give you a better chance to grow into the person God wants you to be. Notice the words "working" and "honestly". Determine to be honest with yourself and to do the work.

SETTING SOME GOALS

Bad, heavy feelings are not permanent. It takes too much energy to keep reliving the past. Now is the time to set yourself some goals; be they ever so short term, get a plan, set out to make it happen.

Plan your work and then work your plan. Is that clear enough? Set some goals for yourself. First, write them down.

As you write out your goals, ask yourself what stands in the way of completing these goals successfully. What can you do to remove these obstacles? How much time will it take? But, Do Write It All Down!

As an example, you need a better job. Is more education needed? Should you go to night school? Do you consider the short-term study plan or sacrifice for the long-term success? Is it worth the price to you? Two years of study versus thirty years of success. It is something to give some serious thought to.

After a divorce, and at 40 years of age, Thomas went to college. He was a maintenance apprentice. At 42 he graduated. He continues to reap the positive rewards of his efforts, through his increased self-esteem, promotions at work, and of course, increases in his salary. The positive time he spent in college, studies, were all contributions to his healing, and his self esteem.

The setting of goals involves every area of your life. Do the same with your physical life. Do you need to lose weight? What is standing in the way? What can you do to change things? Make a chart with these three questions. Again, it's the importance of writing-it-down.

As immobile as you may feel at the present moment; it is time to begin to do something about your life that is productive and rewarding. Remember that you are God's child. Be the best child you can be.

NOTES

CHAPTER SIX

FORGIVENESS
Self forgiveness, Fantasies, How to

"AND FORGIVE US OUR DEBTS, AS WE
FORGIVE OUR DEBTORS." MATTHEW 6:12

Forgiveness is the key to your full healing process in divorce recovery. It may be difficult to understand, very easy to ignore or to look the other way. It is uncomfortable to talk about. But it is an absolute necessity.

There is no getting a full healing without forgiveness. It is not our decision. God commands it. Will you choose to disobey what God has said to do because you are still angry and hurting?

By forgiving you are not saying a wrong has not been done towards you. Nor are you denying the severity of how much you have been hurting or are still hurting. You are saying you have decided to grant pardon for this offense;

this debt owed to you. It is an act of the will, a decision. You fully recognize the hurt but still choose to forgive.

Your feelings have nothing to do with forgiveness. This concept must be understood from the beginning. The principle stays the same, whether you believe it or not. You must decide to forgive in order to have a full healing from the pain and breakup of your marriage.

Without forgiveness you remain tied to the circumstances and the situation. With forgiveness you are freed from the ownership of the problem. Forgiveness breaks that terrible cycle of retribution.

The matter is settled. Everyone is now free to get on with the business of life. Otherwise you continue to rehearse, nursing the hurts, and you never break away from the situation.

Forgiveness is one of the best means of facing the truth about yourself and what really happened to bring about your divorce. You will then be able to work through the problems and become a stronger more wholesome person. To forgive comes from a real position of strength. To forgive provides you a means of moving away from some of the pain of the situation.

Without forgiveness we cannot be where we need to be in Christ, in our relationship with others and with ourselves. Forgiveness begins at the foot of the cross. As Jesus was dying, He asked the Father to forgive those who had hung

Him on that cross. He suffered and died for all those who were to come after Him, including you and me.

In His example of prayer to His disciples, Matthew 6:12, He said, "And forgive us our debts as we forgive our debtors." Where will we be if we do not forgive? We will not be forgiven. If we want our prayers answered, we must forgive those who sin against us.

Forgiveness is costly. Look what it cost the Father God to forgive us. It cost Him His only son.

Forgiveness is love, abundant, infinitely genuine. It is an expression of our will to choose. It is the grace and power to be bold in exercising the opportunity and strength to follow God's direction. We are saved and kept by the work done at Calvary. Why would we choose anything less?

In forgiveness we give up resentment and the desire to punish. We pardon an offense and an offender. The offense may be an emotional happening such as anger, bitterness or envy.

Simply say, "I forgive _____ for their anger, bitterness and envy towards me." "I forgive myself as well as their resulting actions."

We do this willingly as Jesus forgave us.

STEPS TO FORGIVENESS

Be honest about your struggle to forgive. You may not feel like forgiving. It is our will to choose; choose to forgive.

Be honest about your role or your part in the divorce. Your hurt is real just as the struggle to forgive is real. Forget about asking, "What about…?

Forget about blaming and trying to make someone else responsible for what has happened, even if they have a large part of the responsibility. Accept the responsibility only for you. Being honest about your part of the problem is not easy. It does not feel good. We are stuck when our focus is on only what the other party did.

When we are stuck on one sidedness, denying our responsibilities, the problem is magnified. With blaming, growth is not possible. There is no acceptance of personal responsibility. This leaves no need to change or grow. Since you feel you did no wrong, or little wrong, why change anything?

You will carry the same problems you had in the marriage into every future relationship. Everyone, all the time, needs to examine themselves and to make the necessary changes. It's a good thing. Take an honest look at yourself.

The opposite is just as bad, accepting all of the blame. Self-blame always produces self-pity. Responsibility always leads to the opportunity for change, movement and growth.

Isn't that our goal? Our goal is to change for the better, to move forward and to grow into a more wholesome and complete person.

In Psalm 51:3, David was painfully aware of his sinfulness and took responsibility for it through confession and repentance. Focusing on personal responsibility, he received God's forgiveness. David did not blame others, or claim an outraged innocence, pointing a finger at others in self-defense.

It does not matter how guilty the other person is. Would it shock you to learn that the same God who forgives you also forgives the other person? He does not weigh who is the guiltier. He is not wrapped up in "who is to blame."

To help you get started here are some things to start with:

1. Examine what it is you are feeling. Give it its name: rejection, loneliness, anger, abandonment, mockery.
2. Name the people involved. It does not matter who is at fault. We are not to enter into blaming and shaming. You are responsible for how you feel.
3. Name the specific events, one by one.
4. Repeat the process, practicing forgiveness, along with the proper behavior until it becomes a habit. Every day, forgive.

"I forgive_____for_____. I forgive myself for_____.

5. Pray about it.

ALLOW GOD TO FORGIVE YOU

We cannot reinstate ourselves to wholeness. God must do that for us through His forgiveness. Through the death and resurrection of Christ, we are reinstated. It is a gift, free of charge. We have only to ask for it. Acceptance of forgiveness is essential. Accept what God has to offer.

You are forgiven if you feel like it or not because God said so. Your sin can never be too much for God to forgive. It's a fact. Your feelings are not a part of it. Regardless of what you did, or the other person did, the sin is forgivable.

"If we confess our sins, God is faithful and just to forgive us our sins and to cleanse us from all unrighteousness." I John 1:9

FORGIVE YOURSELF

With self-unforgivness you remain connected with the past without allowing it to make changes for the present and the future. Examine your self-talk. Self-talk influences the way we treat ourselves, and how others treat us.

You behave in the exact manner that you speak to yourself. You are the programmer. Tell yourself you are a success and you will begin to act like a success. The bible says, "I will create the fruit of your lips." How do you feed into your thinking and your behavior of unforgiveness?

Self-forgiveness allows you to leave your burdens behind. I can and will begin again is a self-talk that you want to develop.

When things around you are dark and depressing, you may find that you are now saying things you do not really believe, things about yourself, negative things.

These things are not really true. Be positive. In a while you will see that things have changed. Rehearse positive attitudes and behaviors.

I have seen thin people rehearsing "I am fat" until they believe and behave 'fat'. Why would you want to do that to yourself?

God has so many good things in store for us. He places those desires in our hearts, "I am strong. I can do this. I know the way." No matter how much we mature as people or grow as Christians, memories of our own failures rise up to haunt us. This is Satan at his best. The bible says one of his jobs is to be the accuser of the brethren,. We know that as Christians the blood of Christ has covered all our sins.

We are not perfect. We are forgiven. We are more than conquerors in Christ. Accept His love and forgiveness.

Without forgiveness we carry the burden of the offense and it gnaws at our hearts affecting us in all that we do. By keeping anger towards the other person, we give Satan a mighty foothold in our lives and that is exactly what he wants. "Having done all, stand firm." Gal. 5:1

Choose not to worry about the offenses, neither yours nor the other person's. It is a matter of choice.

GIVING UP SOME FANTASIES

Give up blaming the other person. "It's more their fault. They brought this all on themselves." "If I don't talk about it, it will not hurt so much."

These fantasies do not make reconciliation or personal growth easier. They only bury the situation, making it worse later. Sooner or later the issue will rise again and it will have to be faced.

Displacing the pressure through gossip or violent expressions will not ease the pain either. They have no healing properties. Gossip and violence have their own consequences which will also have to be dealt with sooner or later. You will not escape these things. They are fantasies better not entertained at all.

What is finished is finished. Walk with the Holy Spirit to a new place for you.

If your divorced mate remains in your life, make the best of it. You loved them once; there are good points about them too. Concentrate on the good.

It's only temporary anyway. They don't come home with you. Even if it is necessary for them that they remain, forgive and move on. You have a better life waiting for you.

Another fantasy is "I'll get even and then I will feel better." But you won't feel better. "The hurt will go away." It is not so. It must be dealt with or you will continue to be owned by the situations and to living in the past.

"My friends will side with me." This is a way of avoiding responsibility. You need to be concerned with you. It is you that you want to get healed and to grow. Start with yourself and then reach out to others. Comforted...you then comfort others.

Do you have any other fantasies that you are living in hoping that they will carry you through these times? Put them aside. Forgive yourself and forgive the other person too.

What has happened is and always will be a part of you, no matter how desperately we might want to forget the event. We cannot cut out that part of us. The good news is we don't have to.

We are never called to forget. As we forgive and move past the hurt, much forgetting will take place. You will be able to lay aside what has happened and move into a productive, happy life.

FORGIVE OTHER PEOPLE

To forgive is to say, "You are free from my need to hurt you back, my need to seek revenge." "I will not hold you solely responsible for this broken relationship."

We do not have to understand all that has happened. We may be asking ourselves unanswerable questions, such as, "How could someone who loved me leave me?"

Understanding the situation would neither remove the pain nor allow you the freedom to change. You may never understand. So what? Forgive and move on.

The other person's response does not invalidate your forgiveness. They may choose not to accept your forgiveness. Their response keeps them in bondage to the past while your forgiveness sets you free. Their response is not your problem.

You have cleared your side of the slate. Remember that forgiveness is a process. Make every attempt to keep open the areas of communication. Your credibility may be mis-interpreted. It is only important for you to take the proper action. Your actions will have an effect on the actions of others. You are responsible for only your behavior.

HOW TO FORGIVE

Forgiveness is a daily process. It is not a one-time happening. Learn to see the other person as Jesus sees them. He has offered His forgiveness to them also. There is something good about every person, learn to see them in the divine light of God's goodness.

Person by person, offense by offense, you must release them from any debt you think they owe you. There is no "I'll forgive you but not before I let you know how much I hurt." They owe you nothing. The debt is paid in full.

Matthew 6:12, I forgive as I have been forgiven. Unconditional forgiveness is what Jesus gave to us.

When you pray, name the person and event one by one. "I forgive_____for _____. It may take weeks before the heavy emotion lessons. It will lesson. You can count on it.

Our wills are stronger than our memory. Redirect your thoughts to new and positive ways. Release those thoughts to the Lord. Ask God for an alarm system to alert you should you fall back into negative thinking.

When something triggers an area needing forgiveness, remember what you said, you forgive them. In less time than you think, you will deal differently with this issue.

Forgiveness is one of the best tools that God has given us to handle heavy feelings, such as guilt and anger.

Forgiveness sets us free. Confession brings cleansing. Confession brings lightness to darkness.

Be wise in disclosing the facts of your life. The world is smaller than you think. More often than not a far away person will know someone in your immediate circle of acquaintances.

Be careful in whom you choose to confide in. You have your private concerns, which other people do not have a right to know. Your confidant may think others know about your disclosures and feel free to discuss you and your happenings.

Before you act; seek the counsel of the Lord. If you are uncomfortable with any disclosures, keep them to yourself. Push comes to push, seek a professional counselor.

Even if forgiveness is denied you, you have done all that you can. Put the unforgiveness behind you. The problem is no longer yours. Confession admits our humanity, our weaknesses and our imperfection. It admits wrong decisions, indecision, anger and guilt. It is accepting our responsibility in what has happened.

When you forgive, you become a candidate for the supernatural. Forgiveness is love, abundant, infinitely genuine. You then may have grace, power, boldness, truth, opportunity, and strength. They are all there, waiting for you.

By withholding forgiveness we keep our heavy feelings. We give control of ourselves to the other person. They now are in control of how we feel. Their actions determine our feelings and consequently, our behavior.

By forgiving them with unconditional love, you are released from the controlling bondage. You are free to make your own choices.

Learn to consciously say, "I am in charge of how I feel, how I behave. I act rather than react." An indication of your forgiveness is that you have stopped talking about it. It's okay to separate yourself from any unhealthy relationship. Forgive them, and leave. What was so painful before just isn't there anymore. It is not so important to you anymore. You have passed on to other areas. You are free to be forgiven yourself.

In Christ Jesus we are totally accepted and forgiven. Do the same for others. That includes your former spouse.

You act, not react. You have moved on. See what God has done? What you once said about yourself is no longer true. You are a new person.

NOTES

CHAPTER SEVEN

SINGLENESS, SEXUALITY
Making Choices, Sex, Sexual Struggles

"BE KIND, LOVING, FORGIVING ONE
ANOTHER, JUST AS CHRIST JESUS HAS
FORGIVEN YOU." EPHESIANS 4:32

SINGLENESS

Being single is your marital status. It is not your way of life. You get to choose your way of life. You still like to do many of the things you did as a married person. You still like to go to ball games, concerts, watch sunsets, and travel. What has changed is that you are not part of a couple.

Granted, our society is couple oriented in many respects but not in all ways. We learn to be the best in the place we find ourselves. If that place is singleness for the moment, be the best single person that you can be until that status changes.

There is nothing wrong with you because you are single. This feeling of inadequacy feeds yet another assumption that your problems stem from singleness. You are a complete person apart from any romantic relationship you will ever have. Thinking that you are not complete has no bearing on the truth of the matter.

Many important people in the Bible were single. Jesus among them! John the Baptist, Jeremiah, Mary, Martha, Lazarus, Paul; they were all single. Happy singles were doing a magnificent work for the Lord. You are in good company.

FRIENDSHIPS

When we first change our marital status from married to single, it is advisable to establish some strong, same-sex friendships. People you can have a friendship with on a deep level, being intimate, that is, establishing openness, honesty in your relationship.

It is important that you are honest with your friends. Be there for them when they need you and when they don't as well.

Intimacy in friendships includes closeness, familiarity, confidentiality, personal, trust, and acceptance. Over a period of time, friends come more and more similar. It is good to have a special, best friend.

Women tend to make friends easier than men. Becoming a part of a group will help you meet and make friends.

Laugh and cry alike with them. Be the kind of friend that you want them to be for you. They need friends too. When you become that caring person to others, you are beginning to develop a friendship on some solid ground.

Begin to do the right things in your friendships. We say, "we start good, more than we stop evil". Speak truthfully to your friends, build them up, be an encourager to them, and help them physically when they need help.

Get rid of all bitterness, rage and anger, brawling, and slander, along with every form of malice. "Be kind and compassionate to one another, forgiving each other, just as Christ forgave you." (Eph. 4:31). Accept your friends as they are. You're not perfect either.

Your sense of personhood is the source of your happiness. This is a product of your relationship with the Lord, and with yourself and your friends. God does not feel any differently toward you now that you are single.

He loves you in the same way He always did. He knows that all His children make and have made mistakes. He forgives us and helps us to grow through these difficult times.

If you are going to be alive as a single person, you have to care about relationships. It is during recovery from divorce that we need friendships more than ever. Find a group of similar interests. Start your own group. What do you like to do? Do it. Others like to do that too.

Even if your time is now so limited with the need for employment, there are new goals at your place of work. You can be the best, learn new things, look your best, be the 'happy one'. Work on it. Become the person you desire to be.

If it is not working out for you, and it is possible, then leave. Try something new, something else. What would you like to do but never did? Do it now.

Being single can be more of an opportunity for you than an obstacle. This does not mean that you will always be single. Be determined to be the best that you can be until things change,

It does not mean that you are going to sit down and do nothing until someone comes along and makes things different for you. Someone to rescue you from your singleness is not the answer. That can only mean disaster.

We cannot last long in a relationship when we put the responsibility of making us happy on someone else. When we are whole and we bring a whole person to a relationship, then we can begin to think of a stronger relationship than a surface friendship.

We work from where we are, and where we are is, "I am single, recovering from divorce. I have experienced a serious loss. I am moving on."

A major obstacle facing single men and women today is the feeling of not belonging. These feelings can breed insecurity and low self-esteem that are not from God but are from the cultural expectations of our times. The lie from Satan is that "if you were married, you would belong and all your needs would be met. See, everyone is married, especially at your age."

This is a very subtle lie. No one person can meet all of our needs. Only Jesus Christ can meet the needs that rest deep within our hearts. The real issue is not getting our needs met or feeling like we belong, but discovering God's will for our lives and yielding to His love and His control.

It is true that marriage is a blessing, but so is singleness. The single Christian is not bound by the limitations of having a mate and children and is free to develop a mind towards God and His plan for us. Colossians 3:2 applies to everyone: "Set you mind on things above, not on the things that are on earth."

This is where you are. You can make it a better place. You and God together can do great things.

Marriage, when and if it does come, will be sweeter and more fulfilling because the single person has learned to have his or her needs met in the person of Jesus Christ.

A mate is a special gift from the Lord. Bring a whole person to the marriage. For now, live as if you will always be single.

Choose to take care of yourself. Be responsible for you. You can make the most of what is happening now.

CHOICES

Choose to have a quality life. You can develop a quality way of life. Your slate may have some marks and scars on it, but you can live around them. Make your life a constant adventure.

Make a choice to be responsible for your own life, your own happiness, and your own growth. There is life after trauma, heartbreak and stress. Choose to have a quality life. There is life after divorce.

Let today be the day you begin to grow, to reach out for those desires and goals that you hold in your heart. Your singleness may be exactly right for you at this time.

Marriage in itself will not make you complete. If you use your singleness just as a waiting period for Mr. or Miss Right to show up, you are not really getting the most out of your life.

You are allowing yourself to live in a twilight zone, a no-man's land without a vision, a purpose or a meaning. A person without a purpose, a vision, or a meaning is bound to feel discouraged, defeated, and depressed. They will feel worthless. It is time to get on with the rest of your life.

If you are hanging onto a dead relationship, let it go. It is standing between you and your fulfillment. Are you hanging on because you are reluctant to be single?

It may seem easier to you to hang on to a dead relationship rather than face the rejection. Or, are you in a relationship that cannot go anyplace? If you really want more than that, let it go.

It takes strength and courage to let go of a relationship that cannot go anyplace. That relationship keeps you bound up and unable to find a profitable relationship. It keeps you from 'growing on'. Life is too short to remain the same year after year.

Self-pity is counter-productive, and even manipulatory, thinking that the other person may return. Another extreme is hanging on because of continued full sexual intimacy. If the relationship is dead, let it go. There is a better life for you than hanging around something nonproductive and destructive.

Your past is not your enemy. Dwelling on your past can be the enemy. There will always be little reminders and remembrances of people and happenings. We need our past. It is our history, our identity. It will never go away. Keep the good memories, be happy in them.

A bad start can be changed. We are not tied to the past. We do not need to be paralyzed by past mistakes. Release the people in your past from the responsibility of what has happened to you. Along with the Lord, you can be in control of a nourishing and fulfilling life. Events are not always as significant as how we choose to believe they are.

Take a look at what you do in your daily life. Is there a sense of balance? How much time, money, and energy do you spend on nonessential things? What are you doing to remain in the place you are? What can set you free?

We spend a great deal of time, money, and energy on perishable things. How much of these resources do you spend on the part of us that have eternal value? Are you keeping to the old? Are you going to the new? Have you made any new friends?

SEX AND THE SINGLE PERSON

Jim Smoke, author of "Suddenly Single", said it all. "It's a Jungle Out There." There seems to be an assumption regarding singleness that after a person has been married and has enjoyed a sexual relationship, when they become single again, they simply cannot live without sex.

Sex, or the act of having sex, is defined and dealt with by people as a biological function. On a higher level, we have to deal with sexuality as a total package. This package includes intimacy, love, feelings, consideration, kindness, caring, support, and trust. It involves one's whole being. It is involvement with another person that is total and complete; is continuously that way through life.

That is not easy to come to grips with. Ours is a sex-saturated society, i.e. note advertisements, the soap operas, movies, literature. etc.

It is well to note that even though you are single, your hormones and emotions are still working as when you were married. These are normal God given feelings. The challenge is to route these feelings into acceptable Christian directions.

The feelings themselves are in no way wrong. They are like any other feelings. They are feelings we have to deal with in a God directed manner. What does God say about what we are to do?

We need to have friends, pursue goals, and become stronger in our personal lives. It is a natural desire to love and to be loved.

In marriage to love and to be loved gives a strong sense of security. But when we find ourselves single, it often turns to very painful rejection.

You do not have to prove to yourself and to others that you are indeed lovable. You are lovable even if you do not feel it at the moment. Your former spouse must have thought so too when they married you! If at all possible, focus on the immediate goals of your personal growth.

There are many ways to feel and to be loved without sexual involvement. Reach out to others in a worth while manner. Meet a need of theirs. Join a civic or church group. These activities not only fill your extra time but give you much satisfaction and gratification. It is a fulfilling way, for this moment, to meet some of your needs that to you seem to be going unmet.

You cannot build your standards or values on the crowd. The fact that everyone else is doing it is no reason for you to. Having preset standards and values will help you in standing firm regarding your convictions.

Temptations are rarely easy to overcome and to stand firmly against. However, having set your standards, determine to keep them. Tempters, that guy or gal on the make, are everywhere; in the church, in the work place, at social happenings.

We have no sexual rights past the end of our noses. When someone else is used for your own gratification; his or her rights are being violated. Many sexual encounters are simply trips into self-gratification. How long can your needs be met by hurting others?

There are meaningful ways to handle our sexuality. No one has said that it would be easy. The need to establish boundaries, limits in our relationships, allow us to have male, female, married and single friends.

Now more than ever, we need to have friends. Being able to choose for yourself meaningful new relationships will put you on the path to being the person you want to be.

Surround yourself with likeness, people that are supportive, that are and do the things you want to be and do. As you are healing from your divorce process, open the circle of your friends and allow more differences to enter.

Most important, and the first thing you do, establish your standards.

SEXUAL STRUGGLES

Sex is not the same thing as friendship or commitment. The introduction of sex drastically changes the relationship. It increases the vulnerability of both parties. The relationship may appear more secure or deeper than it actually is.

It is wise to remember that sex is never neutral. It builds or destroys. Marriage is the only relationship strong enough to contain its power. Outside of marriage, sex is usually destructive. It almost always causes stress within the relationship.

And, sex outside of marriage is sinful. "Thou shalt not commit adultery." (Mt. 5:27) "The body is not meant for sexual immorality, but for the Lord, and the Lord for the body." Do you not know that your bodies are members of Christ Himself? Shall I then take the members of Christ and unite them with a prostitute? Never! Do you not know that he who unites himself with a prostitute is one with her in body. For it is said, the two will become one flesh, but he who unites himself with the Lord is one with Him in spirit." (I Cor. 6:16-20)

Flee from sexual immorality. Only in marriage is sexual intercourse legal and accepted by God. Because there are special love-feelings between two people does not change that God has permitted sex only in marriage.

Commitment is necessary for real security and intimacy. Using sex as glue for a relationship can only cause you to ask yourself, "Is there, in fact, any real relationship here?" Or, "Are you using sex to patch up a relationship which cannot survive on its own?"

There are many reasons why singles use sex to kill the pain of unmet desires. Some use sex to enhance their moods, to boost their self-esteem, or as an ego booster. It makes them think, "Someone needs or wants me."

Perhaps it is used as proof to the former spouse that you have sexual desires and that you are lovable. Sex is not a toy for personal enjoyment, but is an expression of love and communication between two people.

The way you begin to face sexual struggles is to ask yourself some questions. How do you feel about sexual relations outside of marriage? If both parties consent and are adults, is that all right then?

Maybe it is okay if you are in a meaningful relationship. What does meaningful mean anyway? What about God calling sex outside of marriage sinful? Are you making your own rules now? Are you ignoring what God has said?

What does God think about sex and singleness? Believing sex is a gift from God, it comes with a great deal of responsibility towards the other person involved. It is so much more than meeting your own needs for gratification. Are you of the persuasion that sex is best enjoyed within a marital relationship that also addresses the issue of responsibility and fulfilling the other person's needs?

We have to have solid foundations and well thought through convictions. Again, preset your values and standards. Set your personal limitations prior to the temptation.

Don't be found in compromising situations. You need to set boundaries and guidelines, barriers for yourself. Don't invite your dates up to your apartment, or sit out in dark, parked cars.

What are you doing to change from where you are to where you would like to be? Perhaps, giving yourself some personal limitations would move you to where you would like to be.

Ask yourself what you can do to change what you are doing. Take note of the things you are doing that keep you where you are. Continue to do the positive things that keep you in God's will. Change the sinful things you do, through confession, repentance, to a holy life, giving God the glory.

Deciding you would rather be in another place will not change anything. You must begin to act on that decision. The pleasures of sin are pleasant for the season.

Is what you are doing the best that God intends for you? Getting upset with God because you do not like the boundaries He has set for His people, will not bring you any happiness. Doing your own thing will not help either. Regarding sex, sex is a choice, and choices always bring responsibility.

Talk to God about how you are feeling and where you need help. The Holy Spirit's work is to draw men to Jesus, so you can be sure He is there to help you.

Take comfort that the Lord is there to help you. (Luke 22:31). Get into your bible and read this passage. Satan would have us, but Jesus Himself has prayed for us. Amazing. What a thrill that is to know.

NOTES

CHAPTER EIGHT

SINGLE PARENTING
Games People Play, Children of Divorce

"I HAVE NO GREATER JOY THAN TO
HEAR THAT MY CHILDREN WALK IN
TRUTH." 3 JOHN 4

Feelings do not go away because your marriage is
over. Letting go of your past, your identity with the former
spouse takes time and work. It is a process. It is important
that you begin to focus on the things that make you stronger
today. Concentrate on today.

What kinds of emotions do you have when your former
spouse comes to mind? Anger? Hate? Sadness? Rejection?
Loneliness? Fear? If dwelt upon, these negative emotions
will be destructive to our growth towards a new life.
However, the divorce being final does not put an end to
these feelings. It can be a very confusing and mixed up

time with our emotions being like a roller coaster, which is usually the case.

Your relationship with your former spouse may always be somewhat emotionally charged. What you do with these feelings, these signals,

GAMES PEOPLE PLAY

Frequently both parties will play games with each other. What kind of games do you play?

"I have a date this weekend." (Do you?)

"The kids agree with me." (I'm right, you are wrong.)

"Our friends think that you are a jerk." (I'm okay.)

"The car needs some work done. Can you fix it?" (you owe me.)

Most games are played in order to hang on to the relationship. Letting go may be too painful to do, so you begin playing these games to keep the relationship together. You believe that even hostility and negative reactions are better than no response at all.

You are lying to yourself. Negative and hostile games fail to develop any self-improvements and fail to bring you closer to meeting your goals, even if they succeed in making you feel better at the time.

It is far healthier to accept the fact that you are divorced. You may not have wanted things this way, but this is how they are. Continuous fighting back and forth and baiting the other person is often a form of denial.

It is wishful thinking that maybe we really will get back together. This is not the way to make amends. Accepting the appropriate attitude is to do the best you can for all parties involves. This includes you, the children, and the former spouse.

You will have a much more peaceful time with your ex if you decide to move on with your life. Do not spend your time and energy worrying about what your ex-spouse is thinking about you. Working hard to change your image to meet their expectations only ties you into the pain of the divorce.

Put that time and energy into fulfilling some of your goals. There is no need for you to remain stuck and tied to the past. Begin to develop some skills in a new area. Accept the responsibilities remaining, such as childcare and support, and get on with your life.

There are many broken dreams in a divorce. Dreams you shared with your former spouse. If you focus on them, rehearsing them over and over to yourself and to anyone who will listen, that is not the answer at all. Use that energy to build new dreams. Start believing in yourself again.

Depression and loneliness are often present in a divorce. It may be that counseling is appropriate. How these issues are resolved will affect your relationship with the ex and with everyone else as well.

A neighbor commented on my messy car. My former spouse always had a messy car. In some way, I was unconsciously still thinking, blaming, him for that mess and not keeping the car clean. He had been gone ten years. Wasn't it about time for me to accept the responsibility for keeping the car clean? Once cleaned, I kept it clean. I broke that tie to the past.

Your former spouse does not own the rest of your life. Now is a good time to rebuild your self-concept. It's for you. It is not for anyone else. Your hanging on to the dead relationship after the divorce will hinder your personal growth and may be a barrier to any hope of reconciliation.

In considering reconciliation, the best way to draw your ex-spouse back is to begin getting on with the tasks of your new life as a single adult. Even in really adversarial relationships, courtesy begets courtesy. On the other hand, an outpouring of anger will beget anger, creating an escalation of the power struggle. Didn't you have enough of that in the divorce?

You don't necessarily have to lose relationship with your in-laws. To keep them, you must avoid forcing them to choose between you and your ex-spouse. It may be wise to remember the saying that blood is thicker than water.

Regardless of who is the major party at fault, family usually sticks with family, so do not cause them to come between you and your former mate. Remain the nice person you are and be as friendly and helpful as you were before.

Regarding your former spouse, "Whatsoever things are true, noble, right, pure, lovely, and admirable, if anything is excellent or praiseworthy, think about such things." (Philippians 4:8)

THE CHILDREN

When you became divorced, you did not divorce the children. Determine that they will remain a vital part of your life. Spend time with them; send cards and gifts on birthdays, whatever it takes.

You are the parent so continue to behave like one. Grandparents, do the same. The children are still a part of your family.

Divorce is as difficult for the children as it is for you. They have less experience and learning to draw upon. They experience the same feelings you feel, i.e. anger, hopelessness and sadness.

For their sake, be supportive of their relationship with the other parent, rather than manipulating them away from the other parent. The children most likely love both parents. They form their identity from both parents. Their little world is very unstable right now. They are asking themselves questions but no one is answering them.

Blaming themselves is big on their list of why their mom and dad no longer love each other. They have heard the fighting, the harsh words, and sometimes they seemed to be right in the middle. "Maybe if I were quieter and studied harder, they wouldn't be fighting." "Will we ever be a family?" There is a lot going on in those little heads.

You would do well to take the time to read and study about single parenting and about children of divorce. Strive to be the best that you can be at this time. This requires positive actions.

Avoid using the children as pawns in a nasty game. Consider their feelings and have compassion on what is happening to them through no fault of their own. Your number one goal is to assure them that they are not at fault.

SINGLE PARENTING

Do your best as a single parent. Knowing that there are so many single parent families does not make your job any easier. Raising a child is the most difficult and most important job in the world. Remember, you are a single parent whether or not your children live with you. That doesn't change. You are still a parent.

For the single parent that does not see the children every day, the loneliness may also be magnified. This is where living in the now, being the best you can for the place you find yourself. Get on to a better and more fulfilling life. This is a time you seek God's direction, His purposes, and His constant presence in your daily life.

The children will grow up someday and look back on your divorce with adult understanding. You need only to be the best that you can be. They will see that too.

Life is a balancing act. And for the single parent, the act is even trickier. The only way to keep your balance is to keep your spiritual and mental health. There are many unique challenges a one-parent family faces. Seek the suggestions other single parents may have to pass on to you.

The happiest single parents are those who have taken control of their lives. Be realistic and think positively. They avoid saying, "Poor me." Or "Oh well, there are storms in everyone's life."

At times your problems may seem insurmountable, but to survive, feed yourself with the good you find, the strength you have, and the beauty of your children.

Single parents are the original super moms and super dads. It is not necessary to be so super. Place as much importance on your own mental and physical health as in that of the children. If you are working nights and the other parent want you to baby-sit so that they can go out, you do not need to feel as if you must. It interferes with your sleep, even though you really do want to see the kids that extra time. It is okay to take care of yourself. Explain your situation quietly; simply, just state the facts.

You need and deserve to take care of yourself to survive and to succeed. You need and deserve relaxation, exercise, and solitude. It may take extreme creativity for you to get these things, but the effort is worth it. Becoming ill is the price you pay for driving yourself too hard. Be careful to nurture yourself so that in turn you may nurture others.

For the parent that the children do not live with but do visit regularly, make your home, their home as well. It's okay to have a bike at your house as well as the other parent's house. Make your place as much theirs as you can. Keep their clothes at your house too.

When you plan for their visitation, concentrate on things that include interaction. Do things that allow for conversation, not the things that cause you to sit in a row and watch something. Not that that isn't something you can do too, but not always.

Money can be a really big issue. There are many things a family can do that do not cost a great deal of money. Go to a garage sale; really good buys can be had. You can find toys, board games, clothes, jackets, and all sorts of things. Buy a board game, return home and play the game. Make some popcorn. Plant a garden. Go to a park. The difficultly comes from having to purposely fill the time you spend with the kids; not just letting it happen like when you all lived together.

Your children will learn about relationships by watching how you nurture your friends. Friendship happens when you reach out to others in willingness to share. A healthy social network supports you in times of crisis and also stands behind you when you want to make some life adjustments.

Keep up the moral standards you believe in. Refuse to have any loneliness or depressing times bring you down to a level lower than your standards and values.

Divorced single parents often use the word failure in regard to past relationships. Determine to reject that word along with regret, the cancer of life. Begin to build the new family soul.

What is family? You and the kids are family. Also, the other parent and the kids are family as well.

Time does not heal, although it does take time for healing to occur. Regarding time, you may never have quantity time, so grab the available moment. Let your children know you are all in this together. You will build a sense of unity by working, discussing, playing, and praying together. The conviction that your family is one will make your children feel secure.

People love belonging. The children love belonging, too. Encourage them to keep close to other caring adults and relatives. I have never heard anyone say, "Too many people love me."

Communication with the children is necessary to building a strong, stable relationship with them. Be honest with them. They need to live a life based on realities. The truth, gently told, is best for them but do not burden them with problems they cannot handle, especially those concerning your emotional life.

Invest yourself in where you live. Make it a place you all want to go. They need special places in the noncustodial parent's home. They need their own dresser, clothes, toys, and things that stay in "my house at Dad's." It makes them feel that they are home here too, and not just visiting.

Children need and want boundaries. Consistency provides them with an ordered world that they can understand. Boundaries offer protection, identity, and ownership. It brings them a strong sense of belonging to something.

Hugs, I love you's, and time spent together will counteract the children's feelings of being cheated out of growing up in a home without two parents.

No one has enough time, so we must make time. Decide what is important with the children and then set out together to attain that goal. Beware of those demons that can keep you from your goals. Things like procrastination, perfectionism, fear of saying no, clutter, and preoccupation with the past.

Be as flexible as you can be. Plan B will work too. Why can't you change your plans and do something else instead? Do you have to go to the museum because you have already talked about it? Agree on the change. You are the parent. Do not allow the children to take charge, woek together.

Be the best parent you can be because no one can ever replace you. No One! Cooperate with your former spouse on co-parenting. Both parties need to share the children and establish rules, the goal being to have the children grow into understanding, responsible and realistic adults.

You cannot be both patents, so don't even try. Be what you are and enjoy your home, giving the children love, attention, security, and affection more than ever.

If your ex is resisting you to have a relationship with kids, press on because it is well worth the hassle. You are going to make mistakes, all parents do. Just remember that love and affection will cover a multitude of mistakes. God is always there to help.

This is not the place, being a single parent, to learn by trial and error. There are many professionals, good books, ready to help you on your way. Give your best effort to be the best you can. Avail yourself of the good books, good opportunities available for you.

NOTES

Rev Vogel can be reached at glendavogel@yahoo.com

This material may be used by an individual or as part of the material given in a group setting. The group leader will find it helpful for keeping the group knit together.

It was originally used in a divorce recovery group. The format being: 40 minute teaching, 15 minute refreshments and fellowship, an hour or less in small groups (6 persons or less and a trained facilitator, discussing the subject taught or allowing a member of the group free time to discuss their situation, as needed.) Following the meeting, the group went to a restaurant for fellowship.

As social meetings are so important for emotional health, the group met several times a month, using any excuse to gather together. Home parties, movies, whatever the group decided.

The success rate of these groups saw many people come out of their grief and pain into productive happy lives. Eight members went on to lead similar groups throughout the area.

A professional counselor was available for special needs when needed. The group was encouraged to attend meetings and workshops outside this group as needs presented themselves.